THE BOBA COLORING BOOK
Christmas Edition

Bitsy Boba
where cute and bubble tea meet

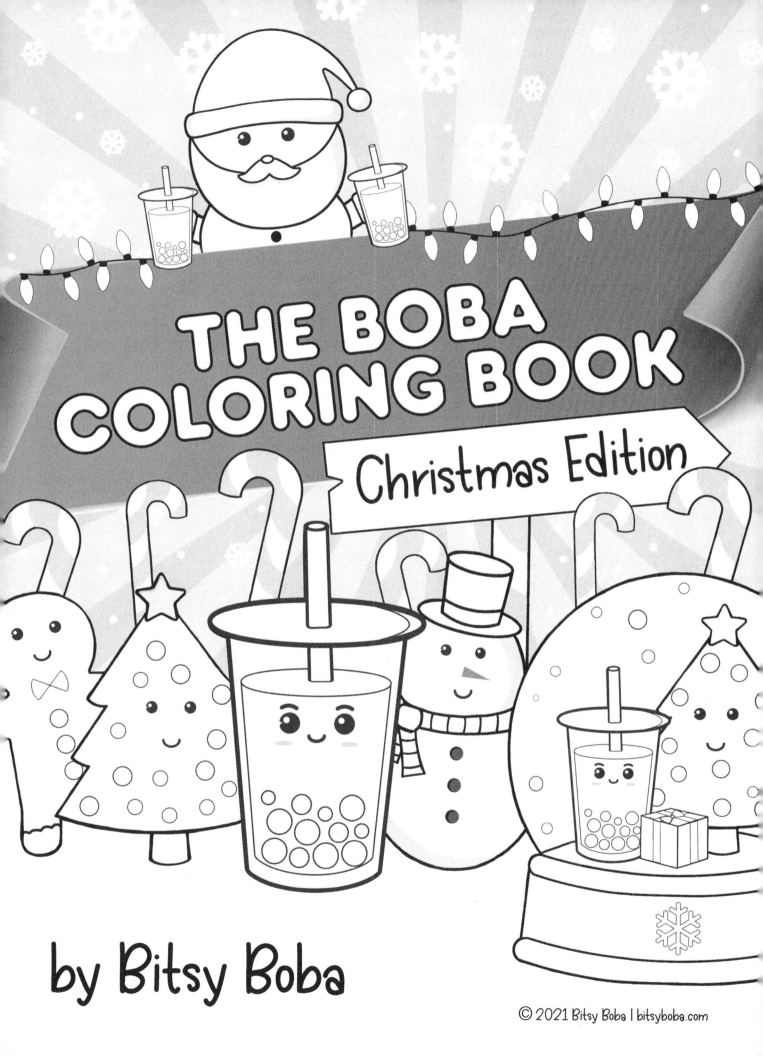

THE BOBA COLORING BOOK

Christmas Edition

by Bitsy Boba

© 2021 Bitsy Boba | bitsyboba.com

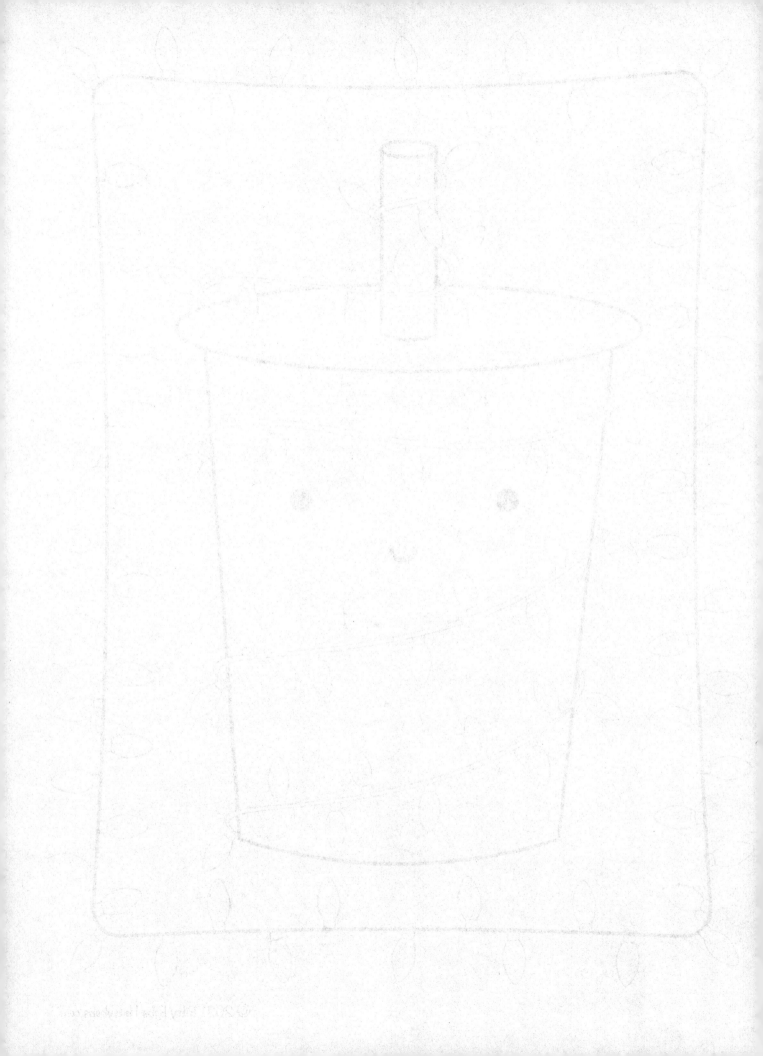

Did You Love This Book?

Here's what you can do to let us know!

♡ **Leave Us a Review**
We greatly appreciate it when customers leave us a positive review. If you purchased on Amazon, visit: www.amazon.com/feedback to write a positive review. If you purchased through our website, you should receive an email with instructions on leaving a review.

♡ **Join Our VIP Club**
Visit www.BitsyBoba.com to sign up for our VIP email list. We'll occasionally send you information about new merchandise, coupons and promotions.

♡ **Free Bonus Digital Download**
As a thank you for purchasing our book, please visit www.bitsyboba.com/pages/bonus to receive a free, bonus digital download of two additional coloring pages.

♡ To order wholesale copies of this book, please email info@bitsyboba.com.

Cover design and book layout by Jennifer Sewell.

Love Boba / Bubble Tea?

Be sure to visit us at www.BitsyBoba.com to shop the cutest boba and bubble tea themed merch, apparel and gifts. We have cute boba designs on everything from T-shirts and sweatshirts to notebooks, magnets and stickers. We add new designs regularly.

Save 15% on Boba Merch

As a thank you for purchasing this book, please use promo code **COLOR15** to save 15% off of our store: www.BitsyBoba.com

Follow Us

Follow us on social media to learn about promotions, giveaways, new products and more. Facebook, Instagram and TikTok: @BitsyBoba

Have Your Artwork Featured

Show us your skills! Tag us on social media in a photo or video showing off your coloring skills for a chance to be featured on our page: @BitsyBoba

Send Us Your Suggestions

If you have ideas for characters we should feature in our next book or on our merch, send them our way: info@bitsyboba.com

About Bitsy Boba

Bitsy Boba is a small, woman- and mom-owned business based in Philadelphia, Pennsylvania, USA. Founded by Michelle, a lifelong bubble tea addict, Bitsy Boba's mission is to create the cutest and most unique boba tea themed merch, apparel and gifts. Boba is more than a drink, it's a lifestyle.

THE BOBA COLORING BOOK

50 Bubble Tea Coloring Pages

Be sure to check out our original, bestselling boba coloring book, *The Boba Coloring Book: 50 Bubble Tea Coloring Pages* which is available on Amazon and our website (www.BitsyBoba.com).

With 50 pages featuring unique illustrations, our highly rated, super cute bubble tea themed coloring book is the first of its kind and suitable for all ages.

Adults, kids and teens all enjoy coloring in these kawaii animals and characters, including:

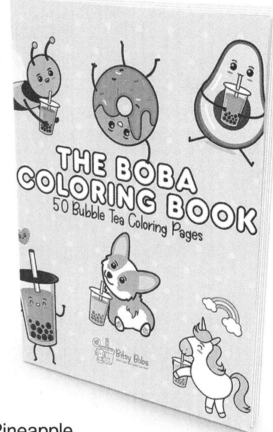

- Tiger drinking tiger milk tea (brown sugar boba)
- Unicorn sipping bubble tea
- Corgi drinking boba tea
- A donut doing a handstand next to boba
- Sushi and boba together
- Kawaii avocado drinking bubble tea
- Boba bear
- Pineapple and boba
- Narwhal sipping boba tea
- Boba and macaron jumping together
- Plus 40 more cute and fun boba coloring pages!

Each page is 8.5" by 11" and features an original, fun and cute illustration related to boba tea with a pattern to color as well. The patterns are simple geometric shapes or relate to the illustration. The back of each page is blank, which prevents bleed through and makes it easy for you to cut out your artwork and frame or share it. You can color using crayons, colored pencils, markers, water colors, paint and more!

The Boba Coloring Book is a high-quality must-have book for any boba drinker, bubble tea lover, milk tea fan or foodie.

Made in the USA
Coppell, TX
13 December 2024

42473179R00063